Three Native American
Learning Stories

This delicate strength
With the breath
of an almost invisible wind,
Lifts Eagle
Far beyond sight.

Paula Underwood
1932 - 2000

Three Native American Learning Stories

Who Speaks for Wolf
Winter White and Summer Gold
Many Circles, Many Paths

and containing additional information
about the nature of a Learning Story

by
Paula Underwood

With Art by Frank Howell

A Tribe of Two Press • Bayfield, Colorado • 2002

A TRIBE OF TWO PRESS
PO Box 133 • Bayfield CO 81122
1-800-995-3320 • www.tribeoftwopress.com

With gratitude, respect, and love,

this edition is dedicated to

Jeanne Lamar Slobod

Advisor, Editor, Enabler, and Friend.

Acknowledgements

A Tribe of Two Press is a publishing firm responsible for continuing to make available the writings of Paula Underwood. We would first like to acknowledge our mother's dedication to the ancient Learning Way reflected in her writings — her grace, dignity, integrity and beauty. We are grateful to be your children.

We also acknowledge the contributions of our ancestors, back through time. Their wisdom and caring for their future children is not lost. We are grateful to be your children.

Jeanne Lamar Slobod has continued to be indispensable to this new generation in sharing wisdom. Bob Helberg again lends his expertise in production and his heart. We would like to recognize the welcoming of this wisdom by many Learners, including those affiliated with The Learning Way Center. Thank you, friends.

Continuing financial support from The Meredith Fund has made this new volume possible.

Finally, we are grateful to every Learner who shares these Learning Stories.

Randy Spencer, Alameda, CA
Laurie Spencer Roberts, Bayfield, CO

Introduction

For the first time, these three ancient learning stories are appearing together within one binding. This is what Paula Underwood intended from the beginning, for together they represent the wholeness of Body, Mind and Spirit. Paula chose to write *Who Speaks for Wolf* first. "It was my favorite story," Paula explained after reading it to me late one cold December afternoon. "It was my first try at writing the Old Things down. I started with *Wolf* because I knew it would be the easiest, and I needed to prove to myself that I could do this."

Long before the other two stories (*Winter White and Summer Gold* and *Many Circles, Many Paths*) were written, Paula referred to the group as "The Three Learning Stories" — I could feel the "t" in "The" being capitalized in her head as she said the words. As each of The Learning Stories was published, Paula wove them into her pattern of presentations, study groups, and retreats. Each provides important lessons in life; together, they provide a way of practicing life in a non-threatening way.

These stories became integral parts of the educational program Paula developed out of the vast ancient wisdom which had been a legacy from her father - and his father - and their Ancestors. Paula's People had used these stories down through the generations as an educational tool. She was not surprised to find that this tradition proved to be effective in our own time as well. She would be pleased, I believe, that the first Tribe of Two publication after her death December 2000, is The Three Learning Stories — together at last.

Early on, Paula had told me each of the stories was designed to illustrate one of the three elements of Mind, Body, and Spirit, but would not say which went with which. Deciding this was to be part of the "learning" experience for the reader. So, in your turn, each of you must make the connection for yourself. To enhance the readers' understanding of the concept of "Learning Stories," several essays Paula wrote (*Central Fire, On the Nature of Learning Stories*, and *Weaving Wisdom from a Learning Story*) have been included in this new volume. In fact, you may want to read these essays before reading the stories themselves.

Paula loved bestowing titles upon her friends. I became her "Enabler in Chief" when I agreed to take on the job of volunteer editor. Actually, it was a privilege to walk in her company and enjoy the friends who gathered around the

Ancient Wisdom which she offered so generously. These diverse supporters of Paula's traditions evolved into a nonprofit organization, The LearningWay® Center with Paula as the head. It was stimulating to brainstorm in such a Circle as to strategies and procedures. When disappointments occurred, as they inevitably did, Paula would say: "Remember, *'That which enables also disables; and that which disables, enables.'*" Life was always substantiating Paula's belief that even failure almost surely might turn into a feast!

And, indeed, that is how it is turning out. Those of us who have worked with Paula are finding ourselves vastly disabled without her wise guidance and her joyous companionship. Yet those involved in the entity she organized also find themselves enabled to carry on with her work by her continuing legacy of Wisdom and are consulting together to determine how best to fulfill the promises made to the Seventh Generation hence.

Paula's children, Laurie and Randy, are the inheritors of both Wisdom and copyrights and they are taking steps to ensure that all of that Wisdom will be preserved as a gift to Earth's children as was specified by Paula's grandfather's grandmother, Tsilikomah.

There is now a growing circle of people across the country and around the world who have learned and benefited from listening to Paula tell her stories and from reading her books. They, in turn, are sharing the Wisdom of the Central Fire with the next generation. This volume is an important step in the evolving awareness which must, and will, become a part of our interconnected lives.

As Paula, herself, always commented as she looked with great anticipation to the future... "Stay tuned!"

Jeanne Lamar Slobod
Georgetown, Texas
November, 2001

Contents

CALLING NAME

At my third winter
My father spoke to me.
He gave me a calling name.
He called me
Turtle People's Child.
And -- when I was tall -- he said
Now you are Turtle Woman

I am called Turtle Woman
And I walk the path my Father showed me.
As he walked it.
As his Father walked it before him;
The path that is always old,
Forever new,
Each life creating
A path that is always the same,
Forever different
From all the others that were
And will be.

So be it
For so it is.

Paula Underwood —
    Turtle Woman Singing

10

Three Native American Learning Stories

My Ancestors, for more than 10,000 years, taught themselves how the human system functions - - from sensitivity to decision. In so doing, they began to see how it was that Many Paths to Understanding were requisite - - some more easily open to This One or That, some so closed that the need for alternate paths became excruciatingly clear.

They saw also how these various paths must be woven together into a whole - - so that the Whole People may prosper.

For that reason, they slowly crafted over many, many centuries complementary learning paths which - - when woven together - - gave memory and access - - wholeness and utility.

As a bridge toward understanding, as a way of practicing life without falling over its cliffs, as a way of honing a keen appreciation of the possibilities and of the wholeness within which those possibilities may be identified . . . the People evolved Three Learning Stories . . . One for each fundamental aspect of this Life Experience . .

One for Body . .

One for Mind . .

One for Spirit . .

Each of these stories is based on an historic circumstance. Each is modified and enhanced to encourage, to create a space in which new learning may occur. Used again and again down through the centuries, they enable each to develop the skills necessary to use Life Experience effectively.

In this way, they function like an access code to the data base that any gathered experience affords. They are like simple-yet-complex piano exercises that enable the later playing of great symphonies.

It is with great joy that we bring you these Three Learning Stories - - Three Strands in the Braid of Life.

Paula Underwood - 1994

Who Speaks
for Wolf

14

Who Speaks
for Wolf

A Native American Learning Story

by Paula Underwood

Almost at the edge of the circle of light cast by Central Fire - - Wolf was standing. His eyes reflected the fire's warmth with a colder light. Wolf stood there, staring at the fire.

A boy of eight winters was watching Wolf - - as immobile as Wolf - - as fascinated. Finally, the boy turned to Grandfather, warming his old bones from winter's first chill.

"Why does Wolf stand there and only watch the fire?"

"Why do you?" Grandfather replied.

And then the boy remembered that he had sat there, ever since the fire was lit, watching the flames - - until Wolf came. Now, instead, he watched Wolf. He saw that it was because Wolf was so different from him, yet also watched the fire, and that there seemed no fear in Wolf. It was this the boy did not understand.

Beyond where Wolf was standing there was a hill - - still so close to the Central Fire that the boy was surprised to see the dim outline of another Wolf face. This one was looking at the moon.

Moon-Looking-Wolf began to sing her song. More and more joined her until at last even Wolf-Looks-at-Fire chortled in his throat the beginnings of a song. They sang for the Moon, and for each other, and for any who might listen. They sang of how Earth was a good place to be, of how much beauty surrounds us, and of how all this is sometimes most easily seen in Moon and Fire.

The boy listened - - and wanted to do nothing else with his life but listen to Wolf singing.

After a long and particularly beautiful song, Moon-Looking-Wolf quieted, and one by one her brothers joined her in silence, until even the most distant - - crying "I am here! Don't forget me!" - - made space for the night and watched - - and waited. Wolf-Looks-at-Fire turned and left the clearing, joining his brothers near the hill.

But I still don't understand," the boy continued. "Why does Wolf look at Fire? Why does he feel at home so close to our living space? Why does Wolf Woman begin her song on a hill so close to us who are not Wolf?"

"We have known each other for a long time," the old man answered. "We have learned to live with one another."

The boy still looked puzzled. Within himself he saw only the edges of understanding.

Grandfather was silent for a time - - and then began at last the slow cadences of a chant. The boy knew with satisfaction that soon he would understand - - would know Wolf better than before - - would learn how it had been between us.

LONG AGO . . .

      LONG AGO . . .

            LONG AGO . . .

Grandfather chanted, the rhythm taking its place with Wolf's song as something appropriate for the forest.

Long ago
    Our People grew in number

        so that where we were
            was no longer enough
Many young men
    were sent out from among us
        to seek a new place
            where the People might be who-they-were
They searched
    and they returned
        each with a place selected
        each determined his place was best

And so it was
    That the People had a decision to make:
        which of the many was most appropriate

Now, at that time
There was one among the People
to whom Wolf was brother
He was so much Wolf's brother
that he would sing their song to them
and they would answer him
He was so much Wolf's brother
that their young
would sometimes follow him through the forest
and it seemed they meant to learn from him

So it was, at this time
That the People gave That One a special name
They called him Wolf's Brother
and if any sought to learn about Wolf
if any were curious
or wanted to learn to sing Wolf's song
they would sit beside him
and describe their curiosity
hoping for a reply

23

"Has it been since that time that we sing to Wolf?" the boy asked eagerly. "Was it he who taught us how?" He clapped his hands over his mouth to stop the tumble of words. He knew he had interrupted Grandfather's Song.

The old man smiled, and the crinkles around his eyes spoke of other boys - - and other times.

"Yes, even he!" he answered. "For since that time it has pleased many of our people to sing to Wolf and to learn to understand him."

Encouraged, the boy asked, "And ever since our hunters go to learn to sing to Wolf?"

"Many people go, not only hunters. Many people go, not only men," Grandfather chided. "For was it not Wolf Woman who began the song tonight? Would it then be appropriate if only the men among us replied?"

The boy looked crestfallen. He wanted so much to be a hunter — to learn Wolf's song, but he knew there was wisdom in Grandfather's words. Not only hunters learn from Wolf.

"But you have led me down a different path," the Old One was saying. "It would please me to finish my first song."

The boy settled back and waited to learn.

As I have said
    The people sought a new place in the forest
    They listened closely to each of the young men
        as they spoke of hills and trees
            of clearings and running water
            of deer and squirrel and berries
    They listened to hear which place
        might be drier in rain
        more protected in winter
        and where our Three Sisters
            Corn, Beans, and Squash
                might find a place to their liking
    They listened
        and they chose

Before they chose
    they listened to each young man
Before they chose
    they listened to each among them
        he who understood the flow of waters
        she who understood Long House construction
        he who understood the storms of winter
        she who understood Three Sisters
    to each of these they listened
        until they reached agreement
        and the Eldest among them
            finally rose and said:
                "So be it - -
                    for so it is"

"But wait"
   Someone cautioned - -
      "Where is Wolf's Brother?
         Who, then, speaks for Wolf?"

But
   The People were decided
      and their mind was firm
      and the first people were sent
         to choose a site for the first Long House
         to clear a space for our Three Sisters
         to mold the land so that water
            would run away from our dwelling
               so that all would be secure within

And then Wolf's Brother returned
   He asked about the New Place
      and said at once that we must choose another
        "You have chosen the Center Place
          for a great community of Wolf"
   But we answered him
      that many had already gone
      and that it could not wisely be changed
      and that surely Wolf could make way for us
        as we sometimes make way for Wolf
   But Wolf's Brother counseled - -
      "I think that you will find
        that it is too small a place for both
        and that it will require more work then - -
          than change would presently require"

But
   The People closed their ears
      and would not reconsider
   When the New Place was ready
      all the People rose up as one
        and took those things they found of value
        and looked at last upon their new home

Now consider how it was for them
  This New Place
    had cool summers and winter protection
    and fast-moving streams
    and forests around us
      filled with deer and squirrel
    there was room even for our Three Beloved Sisters

And The People saw that this was good
  And did not see
    Wolf watching from the shadows!

But as time passed
  They began to see - -
    for someone would bring deer or squirrel
      and hang him from a tree
      and go for something to contain the meat
      but would return
        to find nothing hanging from the tree
        and Wolf beyond

At first
  This seemed to us an appropriate exchange - -
    some food for a place to live

But
  It soon became apparent that it was more than this - -
    for Wolf would sometimes walk between the dwellings
      that we had fashioned for ourselves
        and the women grew concerned
          for the safety of the little ones
  Thinking of this
    they devised for a while an agreement with Wolf
      whereby the women would gather together
        at the edge of our village
        and put out food for Wolf and his brothers

But it was soon apparent
  That this meant too much food
    and also Wolf grew bolder
      coming in to look for food
        so that it was worse than before

We had no wish to tame Wolf

And so
    Hearing the wailing of the women
        the men devised a system
            whereby some ones among them
                were always alert to drive off Wolf

And Wolf was soon his old untamed self

But
    They soon discovered
        that this required so much energy
            that there was little left for winter preparations
            and the Long Cold began to look longer and colder
                with each passing day

Then
The men counseled together
to choose a different course

They saw
That neither providing Wolf with food
nor driving him off
gave the People a life that was pleasing

They saw
That Wolf and the People
could not live comfortably together
in such a small space

They saw
That it was possible
to hunt down this Wolf People
until they were no more

But they also saw
  That this would require much energy
    over many years

They saw, too
  That such a task would change the People:
    they would become Wolf Killers
  A People who took life only to sustain their own
    would become a People who took life
      rather than move a little

It did not seem to them
  That they wanted to become such a People

At last
  One of the Eldest of the People
    spoke what was in every mind:
    "It would seem
        that Wolf's Brother's vision
          was sharper than our own
  To live here indeed requires more work now
      than change would have made necessary"

Grandfather paused, making his knee a drum on which to maintain the rhythm of the chant, and then went on.

Now this would be a simple telling
  Of a People who decided to move
    Once Winter was past

Except
  That from this
    The People learned a great Lesson

It is a lesson
  We have never forgotten

For

> *At the end of their Council*
>> *one of the Eldest rose again and said:*
>>> *"Let us learn from this*
>>>> *so that not again*
>>>>> *need the People build only to move*
>>>> *Let us not again think we will gain energy*
>>>>> *only to lose more than we gain*
>>>> *We have learned to choose a place*
>>>>> *where winter storms are less*
>>>>>> *rather than rebuild*
>>>> *We have learned to choose a place*
>>>>> *where water does not stand*
>>>>>> *rather than sustain sickness*

"Let us now learn to consider Wolf!"

And so it was
  That the People devised among themselves
    a way of asking each other questions
      whenever a decision was to be made
        on a New Place or a New Way
  We sought to perceive the flow of energy
    through each new possibility
      and how much was enough
      and how much was too much

Until at last
  Someone would rise
    and ask the old, old question
      to remind us of things
        we do not yet see clearly enough to remember

"Tell me now my Brothers
  Tell me now my Sisters
    Who Speaks for Wolf?"

And so Grandfather's Song ended . . . and my father's voice grew still.

"Did the boy learn to sing with Wolf?" I asked.

"All may," my father answered.

"And did the People always remember to ask Wolf's Question?"

My father smiled. "They remembered for a long time . . . a long time. And when the wooden ships came, bringing a new People, they looked at them and saw that what we accomplish by much thought and considering the needs of all, they accomplish by building tools and changing the Earth, with much thought of winter and little of tomorrow. We could not teach them to ask Wolf's question. They did not understand he was their brother. We knew how long it had taken us to listen to Wolf's voice. It seemed to us that These Ones could also learn. And so we cherished them . . . when we could . . . and held them off . . . when we must . . . and gave them time to learn."

"Will they learn, do you think, my father? Will they learn?"

"Sometimes wisdom comes only after great foolishness. We still hope they will learn. I do not know even if our own People still ask their question. I only know that at the last Great Council when we talked about the Small Ones in their wooden ships and decided that their way and our way might exist side by side - - and decided, therefore, to let them live . . . I only know that someone rose to remind them of the things we had not yet learned about these Pale Ones.

"He rose and he reminded us of what we had already learned, of how these New Ones believed that only one way was Right and all others Wrong. He wondered out loud whether they would be as patient with us - - once they were strong - - as we were now with them. He wondered what else might be true for them that we did not yet see. He wondered how all these things - - seen and unseen - - might affect our lives and the lives of our children's children's children. Then to remind us of the great difficulties that may arise from the simple omission of something we forgot to consider, he gazed slowly around the Council Circle and asked the ancient question:

"TELL ME NOW MY BROTHERS
TELL ME NOW MY SISTERS
WHO SPEAKS FOR WOLF?"

Winter White
and
Summer Gold

44

Winter White
and
Summer Gold

A Native American Learning Story

by Paula Underwood

All of the leaves
    on all of the trees
        were particularly soft that spring

New shoots of all the varying grasses
    burst through the crusted, yielding earth
        each small fissure forming a minute valley
            out of which this new life sprung

Waters began the soft sounds of spring
    Winter White
        melting into the clarity of fresh water
        seeping through earth to thickening roots
        gathering into cascades
        renewing their long trek to the sea

There was joy
    Among the People
Earth began a new song
    and the People
        voiced her melody

Those who had been restrained
  by the deepening snow
    sought the freedom this new warmth afforded

Steeped in the exuberance of unrestrained motion
  some of the people
    already found their way to that part of Earth
      which would yield Summer's gift
    exploring last year's clearing
    seeking with probing sticks
      the nature of the soil
        soon to receive
          the gathered future of the People

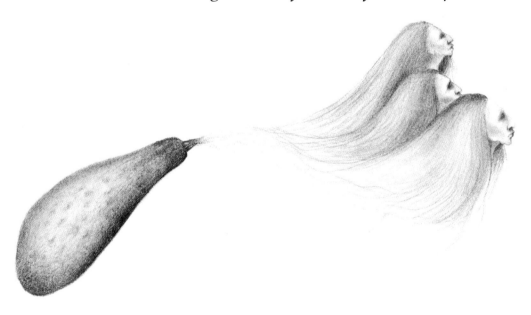

Some other of the People
    were already among the trees
        slowly convincing them to make way
            for our Three Sacred Sisters
For after this Spring comes another . . .
    and, after that, a third

And surely
    only those Peoples
        who understand the sequence of Summers - -
            encouraging trees toward corn - -
                gift Earth's children with our Summer Gold

New waters swelled in every stream
    cracking and carrying off winter's icy coat
Almost with the sound of the first crack
    small boys appeared at each stream edge
        sharpened stick lances poised
            in search of slow moving fish
        eager to find them
            before their winter sluggishness
                washed away with the spring waters

Soon
    the stream-side trees were festooned with nets
        rapidly filling with the sudden fruit
            of these same spears

Each valiant hunter
    maintained his silent concentration

Yet
    when any net filled and was taken down
        cries echoed through the forest
            as the swollen nets made their way
                from stream to prepared earth

"Hoy Hoy - -
Look this way"
- - a young voice cries - -
"Ya-a-ah Hoy - -
Spirit listens"
- -comes the answer - -

And the trees at the edge of forest clearings
rapidly acquired the look of stream-side trees
The pungence of fish too far from water
increasingly filled the forest air

Now
  the women had come to the clearings
    singing songs of earth and warming air
    songs of thanks, also,
      for the netted fish . .
      for the life they would bring
        to the quickening corn

They sang:

  "From Earth the water comes

  "From waters the finned swimmers come
    Gathered in nets
    Swimming in that way through air
    They swim now through earth
    And accompany our Sacred Sisters

  "May each green stalk
    Rooted in earth and water
    Remember the gift of fish"

Somewhere beyond the hill
men searched the earth
for indications of life

This early in the warming of Earth
only certain of our Brothers were sought - -
their four-footed marks
showing us their direction

Like certain fish
many others were neither sought nor found - -
their participation in the Great Earth Dance
in the beginning of new life
being preferable to the People

No one
concerned themselves with the houses

During the deep snow
all of the customary renewal was undertaken
clothing mended or begun
panels within the houses replaced
worked bone and shell patterns
set with careful stitches on ceremonial dress
ancient patterns strung once more
with fresh new thongs

Then later- -
after the season of growth - -
thoughts would turn to the houses themselves
supports would be again secured
thongs woven, wrapped, and wet with stream water
would shrink slowly under watchful eyes
securing each joint against unexpected change
bark panels would be placed against these joints

"Let the house be secure as a water carrier"
   - - some of the men would sing - -

"As no water drips from a well-made basket
   Let no water drip through this well-made roof"

And
   there would be laughter as one told another
    that the heads in his family
     surely would be damp long before spring
      corn perhaps sprouting from someone's pocket
       long before it sprouted from any earth

And with laughter
And with song
And with mutual admonitions
   to take greater care
    this task, too
     would be well accomplished

But now
  the houses stood empty of their inhabitants
    Neither side of the walls
      received any patient attention

The world outside was stirring

Last winter was difficult

A winter of too much snow
  followed a summer of too little rain

Little kernels of future life
  had been carefully stored
    preserved as one preserves the future
      of a Whole People

During the winter
  no one asked for this corn

  Not one cry was heard
    even from the smallest of the People

  Each morning began with a song
    from She Who Adjudicated within each Long House

"Great One, we give thanks
*   For the bounty of Earth*
*   For her kindness to us*

"Great One, we give thanks
*   For the wisdom of the People*
*   Who preserve the seed of Future Life*

"Great One, we give thanks
*   There is little . . .*
*   But there is enough"*

Quiet murmurs were heard among the People
   gentle echoes of purposefulness
      and then . . .

      "Snow Soup!"
         - - someone called - -

And laughter drowned the footsteps
   of those who were young
      as they danced out through the door
         to gather fresh snow
         filling each water carrier with snow to be heated
            for of wood there was truly enough

While the Snow Gatherers fulfilled their purpose
    many women counted again
        the carefully preserved bounty
           of last summer's drying earth
        dividing each kind
           into the same number of portions
                as there were days left until spring
                    and people left who were hungry

Each Snow Gatherer
    received a portion of berry cake, however small
        as a gift for this gift of fresh snow
    According to each individual nature
        they would swallow quickly . . .
    or munch slowly . . .
    or save for later in the day
        enjoying the knowledge of this tasteful wealth
           to be consumed at will

But surely
   each one ate or drank or saved and later enjoyed
      this usual beginning to each day
         understanding the sore mouth sickness
            that might otherwise come
         wishing health for themselves and others

Later in the day
   one or more of the Three Sacred Sisters
      greeted them from the cooking pots - -
         Corn or Beans, sometimes Squash
Even with such limited stores
   the women in each Long House
      managed variety in every meal

The favorite winter places to dig under the snow
   for fresh roots and occasional leaves
      were carefully husbanded
         portioned slowly through the winter as a reminder
            that Spring, after all, would come
And dried herbs, those memories of Spring
   were kept through the winter
      varying the flavor of every dish

This was the time
   for the smaller boys whose lighter weight
      might not break through this crust of snow

They set snares
   for an occasional squirrel
Dug tunnels
   from one house to another
Searched under trees
   for nests of sleeping furred creatures

These small gifts of fur and food
   were appreciated by all

"We will feast"
   - - the women cried - -
      carefully cutting each portion
         into the simmering pot
      sharing even the smallest such gift equally
         with all the people within that Long House

And
  songs would be sung to the brave hunter
    who had attained, perhaps, his seventh winter
      along with one more squirrel

Sometimes
  one such hunter might not return

  His path would be sought
    by those taller than the snow
  And carefully built tunnels would disappear
    beneath the flailing feet
      of those who hunted the hunter

  Found at last
    on the other side of a collapsed tunnel
      he would ride home
        on shoulders glad at the weight
      protesting all the while the destruction
        of too many snow passages

The young girls
　　disappeared with equal frequency
　　　　down such snowy passages
　　　　　　seeking the company of others
　　　　　　seeking their own first winter digging places

　　　　Even grass roots might be welcome
　　　　　　in a winter which left the People leaner
　　　　　　　　as the days progressed

Happy songs
　　were sung to any such
　　　　who returned
　　　　　　with food for the simmering pots

　　　　"Here is one who understands
　　　　　　The needs of the people around her

　　　　"Unbidden, she seeks winter's cold
　　　　　　And returns with memories of Spring

　　　　　　"We feast . . .
　　　　　　　　We feast . . .
　　　　　　　　　　We feast"

And so the winter passed - -

Sometimes
    the women would decide to ask a small band of men
        to search the woods for a larger one
            among our four-footed brothers
                who might join our Three Sisters
                    dancing with them in the cooking pot

But in such a winter - -
    with such snow and wind - -
        they would see how easy it was
            for fewer to return than those who left

    Understanding this
        it would seem to them that a lonely stomach
            is preferable to a lonely heart
    And
        they would speak against such missions

And yet
    the men - - seeing the thinning faces - -
        would go out from time to time
            searching the whitened woods
        or sit cross-legged on a frozen stream
            searching through the ice
                for those finned swimmers
                    still moving through the blue-black waters

In the shallower streams
    ice was cut and melted
        yielding not only water for washing
            but a finned swimmer here and there - -
        frozen in ice

And again
    Whatever came home in the hands of the hunter
        however small, however large
            was greeted with the same joy
                equally apportioned among all the fires
                    within that large and loving home

Cries of
  "We feast . . .
    We feast . . .
      We feast"
beat against the soft panels
  that divided the rooms one from another
    and echoed against the walls

"Let the cold and dark
  remain outside"
    - - the echoes seemed to say - -

"Let the warmth and joy of family
  remain within"

And yet another thing occurred

During a scant winter
  no matter how small the gift
    from forest or from stream
  some portion
    was cut and hung in the smoke of the fire

"Here is Tomorrow"
  - - she who wielded the knife would cry - -

And
  all felt grateful
    to see this evidence of care - -
    this gift to the next day's need
      suspended before their eyes

"My eyes keep my stomach full"
  - - someone would laugh - -

"Were I as tall as you"
   - - some very young one might add - -

"My stomach, too, might seem full - -
   but my eyes
      are too distant from tomorrow's supper
        to fill my stomach"

It was said with dignity
   and the reply was equally quick

"To each in equal measure"
   - - one of the women would gently remonstrate - -

"More Snow Soup, quick"
   - - someone else would cry - -

And
   a young stomach
      none too happy with its contents
        would soon be at least full - -
      at least warm - -
   the next meal never too far off

"But if they were hungry, my Father, shouldn't they be fed?" I asked the one who sang this song.

"If they are fed more today and less tomorrow, where is the value?" he asked in return. "If their stomach grows larger with today's meal and even smaller with tomorrow's, will not their pain be greater?"

He paused, allowing me time to consider these alternatives, and then went on. "What, after all, is the purpose here?"

Through my mind flashed pictures of forest . . snow . . stream . . fire . . a Long House with people living together inside, surviving yet another winter. At last I saw the image.

"They are surviving," I replied. "All of them are surviving . . . every one. This is why the women do not encourage the men out in such difficult weather. A full stomach is not an equal trade for an empty space by the fire. Nor even . . ." I considered further, remembering all my father had said about cold and snow, chill winds and beating ice crystals. "Nor even the burning of the fingers caused by too much cold!"

A slight smile touched the corner of his mouth . . . blending slowly with the sharpened look of greater concentration. "Perhaps something else concerns you," he suggested.

I saw at once the puzzled frown that still divided my eyes, one from the other.

"Should they not, my Father, should they not give more to the children? Are they not the Future? Do not bones still grow and legs lengthen? Should they not have more of the offered food?"

"Consider what you have already learned," he replied.

And I considered, searched the forest with puzzled eyes, saw snares and tunnels, ice-sitting men and purposeful hunters. Nothing here answered my concern.

The bark-covered walls of the Owachira appeared before me, secure against the intrusion of snow, even snow mounting to the roof. I saw at last through these walls into the heart of the Long House, each family compartment set against the walls, partitions between them of woven saplings covered now with winter panels of soft worked skin. I saw the Central Fires down the center passage, wider than a hall, perhaps as wide as our living room. I saw Tomorrow hung in the smoke of each fire and felt hunger of my own, thinking those suspended strips of nourishment might find a happier home within my empty interior.

"Snow Soup, quick!" I heard someone cry . . . and the warming liquid cascaded down my throat, leaving a full but somehow unsatisfied stomach. With eager eyes I watched the women preparing the dancers for today's simmering pot.

"Not too long to wait," a voice next to me said. And I looked up, startled, at the hunter next to me. It was the man whose eyes filled his stomach. He was so tall he seemed to disappear into the ceiling. I saw at last the smile on his face — the same patient smile I saw so often beneath my father's questioning eyes.

I understood that love.

"Which of these women is my mother," I asked.

"They all are," he replied. And I understood him. For surely all the women in that Great House shared responsibility for each person within.

"No burden is too great," my father had said, "when many shoulders lift it."

But the Tall Hunter was speaking again. "If you have not yet chosen a mother," he said, "share mine," and he sat down beside me.

The freedom of each child to choose parents they might prefer raced through my mind, each step slowly taken, always in consultation with She Who Adjudicated within that Great House. For the first time I understood the implications.

"You see how it is," his hand swept out in indication. "This One is my mother, as I am her son. She will give to each of us from her simmering pot."

The woman ladled from basket to dish, handing the first dish . . . and then the second to her son. One of these he handed, in turn, to me.

74

I was on my knees in an instant, peering from his dish to mine. "They are the same," I said with no small astonishment. "But . . . but . . . you're so much *bigger* than I am!"

"Do you have an answer?" my father was asking.

The Long House disappeared around me. Mother of Hunter was already gone.

"Oh, don't go!" I cried out to the Hunter. But he smiled at me - - that same smile - - and was gone.

"I would be willing," the sadness in my voice lengthened to a sighing sound, "to have an empty stomach in order to live in such a house."

"I hear part of the answer, my Daughter. Now find the rest."

"He was bigger than me," I answered. "Much, much bigger. But his mother gave us each the same . . . exactly the same."

"Is that not in the manner of the People?" my father asked.

"But don't you see?" I asked with the untempered impatience of youth. "If he's so much bigger than I am, yet receives the same from one who is his mother more than mine . . . am I not given more?"

"You have the rest of your answer," my father smiled, "and more. For even those who count many, many winters and whose years weigh them down to a smaller stature, even these ones receive equal measure with the tallest hunter. It is the way we show respect for age. We have understood its value for a very long time."

Seeing no further questions in my eyes, my father settled back again and began the sonorous, rhythmic tones with which each Telling begins . . and recommences.

I have told you
  - - he intoned - -

  How it was for our people

Snow so deep
  that some mornings
    the long poles were necessary
      to clear the smoke holes in the roof

Snow so deep
  that after the storm
    the only incoming air
      filtered through that snow
  And once the smoke holes were cleared
    wall flaps were lifted
      revealing a second wall of snow

But

    snow sits in little bright crystals . . .
      and air passes easily through it . .
        unless by carelessness . .
          someone has allowed this access to air
            to thaw and then freeze again
  For I tell you now
    a wall of ice permits little transit of air

And so
  the women kept the center warm

But
    the compartments against the outside walls
      were kept cool to discourage thawing
  Even did some families move
    from this compartment . . and that one . .
      joining other families
      joining warmth with warmth

Then these uninhabited rooms were kept closed
    soft skin panels
        shielding such interiors
            from the warmth of fire
        securing access to air

And
    each such access was regularly checked
        to assure that no ice walls had yet formed
    Any such were dug away to soft, crystal snow
        with its gentle filtered air

For
    the well being of the People
        comes in many forms - -

That Which Is Consumed
    finds Two Paths
        toward energy and strength

The nature of Earth
  is filtered through her creatures
    toward the bubbling dance of each cooking pot
    toward each daily need

Even so
  is the nature of Sky
    the clear, ambient air
      filtered through snow crystals
        toward each Central Fire
      toward the rising and falling of breath
      toward each and every daily need

Such are the two paths

Now

    This same winter

        of snow tunnels and snares for squirrels,
        carefully husbanded food and Winter digging
        snow filtered air and smoke trails in the sky

    This same winter

        was a winter of such bitter cold

            that not even the line of Central Fires

                in each Long House seemed enough

    Not even

        the Winter Robes prepared so lovingly

            by the women for their families

                from the gifts of Bear and Fox and Rabbit

    Not even

        the covered walls around the People

            kept out the cold

Little hunting was possible

Even snares set for squirrel were rapidly buried
    hidden by the new snow
And tunnels collapsed of this new weight
    the intrusion of no Hunter's foot even necessary

This same winter
    All the earth seemed frozen
        In a long wait for spring

On the rare days when wind and snow allowed
    few tracks were found
        and even these few were rapidly lost

No new gift found its way
    into the dancing waters of any bubbling pot

The women counted each mouthful of food
    thinking now of the possibility
        of a late spring and a hungry People

Now
  they told each other - -
    it is time for the sometimes food

And
  plans were laid
    for the gradual inclusion of foods
      that might otherwise not be eaten

Bark was peeled from many appropriate trees
  and the layer beneath carefully stripped away
    to slowly add to each cooking pot

"Share the Earth with me, my Brother"
  - - each gatherer explained to birch and elm - -

"I leave enough for you
  but without this gift
    there may be none of the People
      to dance beneath leaf-covered branches - -
        and think how much sorrow that would bring!"

Oaks were searched
   for any clinging acorn
A few crumbs of food
   were left here and there near snares
      for the smallest of the four-footeds
Even these were joyfully greeted
   and quickly shared by the cooking pots

But
   the seed corn was kept . .

And
   the promise of Tomorrow
      still hung over the fire . .

And
   berry cake was still enough to last
      - - day by day - -
         toward a possible spring

Now

> *when I tell you this*
>> *you will remember*
>>> *how each Long House is built . .*
>> *out of poles and bark, furs and woven reeds*
>>> *and here it is*
>>>> *that the People find last food*

For

> *when each attainable oak has been searched*
> *each bush deprived of its last winter berry*
> *each under-bark strip brought to the bubbling pot*
>> *as a gift from forest to the People*

Then

    do eyes turn to the nature of the House itself - -
      underbark is stripped from remaining poles
      some skins may be boiled
        for the last residue they contain
      reeds may be soaked
        and mashed into a digestible gruel

And

    although the People might design no feast
      along such lean-year lines
    During such years
      they are glad of even such resources
        and sing their inclusion
          into the dance of life hung over each Fire

My Father's voice grew still once more and my thoughts stretched out to encompass all he had said.

The bitterness of bark touched my thoughts . . and reeds pounded into a bread-like mass - - The unsatisfying warmth of Snow Soup filled my stomach once more - - touched, now, with the tang of boiled skins.

Providing for the future as they knew how to do, I understood each pot would contain the dance of a little corn, some roots, some beans - - reminders of the plenty that lay ahead. And now the persistent thuck, thuck of the pounders sounded within the House - - reminders of the patient care the women took of each and every person, encouraging the pith of bark and reed toward the possibility of digestion.

I saw how a People might sustain themselves past probable survival. Working together, each individual purpose sustaining the common goal, many feet followed a path that few alone might not survive.

I remembered the concern of others for my well being that somehow filled me along with the Snow Soup, and I saw how much farther a little will carry you when there is love in the House.

"It is the rest of the story," I said out loud. "The greatest flavoring for any food is love. The survival of the People requires love as well. It is the third step round the circle, the gift we add to Earth and Sky, the completion of our purpose."

"And no purpose beyond?" my Father asked.

I considered the nature of the circle the People danced . . . Earth and Sky and the Unity expressed as Love . . I saw the walls of the Great Long House, bubbling pots filled with dancing Sisters . . . or Snow Soup . . .

I saw . .

But I had never *seen* any such House! This image, which held for me all the clarity of constant association, I had built with the bark and poles of my father's words. Every corner I could look into - - and *know* what was there - - came from his patient answers to my many questions. It had been a long time . . a long time since any in my family had stepped within the structured walls of any Long House. And yet I saw the image, patiently transferred from generation to generation, as if I were my grandfather's grandmother.

"Why did you do it?" I asked .. and met my father's startled gaze. "Why did you listen and learn so patiently about something you never saw? Why do you sit with me now and explain until your legs no longer straighten when you stand?"

His startled gaze slowly softened into a smile.

"I was wondering," he answered at last, "what you have learned from this?"

And then I understood.

A way of life both he and I thought beautiful had been preserved. So clear in his mind and in mine that we could have built such a House, established such a People. No day passed but that we borrowed some Ancient Wisdom - - passed from generation to generation - - and understood more clearly our present circumstance.

"In our own way," I answered him, "we also sustain the People. We listen to the things they learned, thread them on the cords of our own thoughts, hold them close to the fire of our own vision, and suspend them at last in the smoke of our understanding .. preserving them for tomorrow.

"Through us, the People have survived more than

the coldest Winter. Through us they have survived the centuries."

I was quiet for a long time, listening to the person I would become.   Listening to my own grandmother-voice which one day would speak so that others might learn.

At last my Father's words entered the silent space between us.

"I see understanding," he explained, "where before I saw only questions . . . I see learning."   Again he waited until the inward turn of my thoughts gradually changed direction, becoming a willingness to listen.

As my eyes turned toward him, he began once more the rhythm of the chant, fingertips beating slowly . . against his folded knee.

I would be pleased to tell you
   that our Brother, Bear, suddenly appeared
      and offered himself to the People
         But it was not so

I would be pleased even to tell you
   that Beaver or Otter
      walked up to the door of our Long House
         to offer himself to the dancing waters
            But neither was this so

The many last days of Winter
   continued as they had begun
      filled with Snow and Driving Wind
   Sad, indeed
      for any who sought new possibilities
         for a dwindling store of food

And yet
*   there was laughter in the House - -*

One Hunter met another with the admonition
*   "I thought you were a much larger man*
*   than you presently seem to be!"*

*   "Like Bear who sleeps all Winter"*
*   - - he replied - -*
*   "I need the warming sun of Spring*
*   to expand my shrunken Winter Self"*

And
*   all would laugh at the image of this man*
*   shrunk small with Winter cold*
*   suddenly expanding under a warming sun*

*   "Perhaps if you sit close enough to Fire . . ."*
*   - - some one suggested - -*

And again . .
  rafters peeled bare of bark . .
    rang with the sound of merriment

Even those working outside the House
  peeling back the last bark covering
    from its many poles
      maintained the pattern . . .
        stitching together one person and another
          through the mutuality of laughter

"Tell me, my Brother"
  - - one of them asked - -

"Will next Winter be a happier time than this?
  - - and he rubbed his stomach
    to make his concern even more evident

"Look at it this way"
  - - his companion answered - -

"Perhaps next year
we will think back over this Winter
cooking pots filled with boiling bark
the distance around each waist
growing smaller and smaller
and think . . .
how lucky we were to have so much bark!
for surely
next year there will be none left."

And
he leapt down from the roof of that Long House
the last of the bark clutched in his hand
and ran through the House singing

". . . This year's plenty . . ."

And dropping an equal portion
of the bark retrieved
in each of the dancing waters
suspended over the Central Fires
which dotted the length
of the central hall

There was much merriment that day

For
 the People held a celebration
  in honor of this New Wisdom

"We have more than we know"
 - - they called it - -

and they danced quietly
 the beginning of the Spring
  they all searched for in their hearts

And from that day

 The People counted three more
  until the snow outside
   was a little shorter than before . .

And three times three
　　until a young boy came back from the stream
　　　　struggling his way through the softening snow
　　　　　to call out to all the People
　　　　　　the first signs of cracking ice

And
　　all the young boys rushed outside
　　　　to search for new wood
　　　　　for sharpened stick lances
And
　　all the young girls toiled patiently once more
　　　　over the nets that would soon festoon
　　　　　the stream-side trees

For I tell you now
　　this was that very Spring
　　　　when the leaves were especially soft . .
　　　　and when the Earth herself
　　　　　seemed eager to split apart
　　　　　　encouraging all the new spring grasses

And

 when the first shoots of green corn
  appeared through the folds of Earth
   the People celebrated as never before - -
feet grown slowly stronger
  sounded their thanks on the Earth
   echoed in the constant beating of drums
    which were sacred to this purpose

And

 many voices rang through Elm and Birch
  who, with their bark
   had also enabled this celebration - -

When at last
 the People had, indeed, expressed their joy
  in things growing again
   one among them rose to speak

"You have seen how it is
  my Brothers, my Sisters

You have seen how a lean winter
  may be followed by a winter
    which is leaner yet . .
  And how the summer between
    may be of little benefit

"Let us now resolve
  to learn from this

  "Let no summer pass
    which is full of ripening Corn
      when none is saved
        for the following Winter

  "Let no summer pass
    which is full of ripening Beans
      when none is saved for the Winter
        that follows after that

"Let no summer pass
    that is full of ripening Squash
        when none is saved
            even for the Third Winter

"Let us not again
    peel bark from lodge poles
        for want
            of First Winter preparations

"Let us not again
    See the young among us
        shrink slowly before our eyes
            for want
                of Second Winter preparations

"Let us not again
    chance the well being of the People
        for want
            of Third Winter preparations

"From this day forward . .

"Let us choose to be a People
prepared for no less
than three difficult years

"Let us choose to be
a People who survive
even the Third Winter"

"And from that day to this," my father went on, "The People have always saved from summer's bounty more than One Winter requires - - more even than Two Winters might require - - enough at last for the Third Winter.

"Even in this land of Things Grow in Winter .. even here .. you and I save something for the Third Winter."

And it was so - -

For even though our garden grew throughout the year under the California sun, in the back of our kitchen pantry always lay Corn my father and I had dried .. and Beans and Squash . . . and the cans of tuna fish I also thought appropriate.

"A new friend to join our Three Sacred Sisters," my father chuckled. And the cans of tuna were gathered from our grocery box in much the same manner as we gathered Corn from our garden, then placed with ceremony at the back of the pantry shelf which was sacred to us.

Now you might think that . . living in a land of Winter plenty . . none of these things we kept so carefully would have any other purpose. But I tell you now it was not so.

For the time was such that my father . . who walked the second story beams of houses being built . . found no more such houses to build. And the times were such that our Three Sacred Sisters - - Corn, Beans, and the seeds of Pumpkin - - found their way into the soil of our Winter garden, sustaining life.

And my cans of tuna fish . . one by one . . came down from our pantry shelf to provide our Sunday dinner.

"Better than bark," my father proclaimed and sang from time to time during each such meal a song of thanks for such wisdom.

All but three of those cans were gone before my father found work again. And for those three we had designed a different purpose.

"We give . . and we take from Life," my father said. "If we forget to give . . we have forgotten too much."

And so those three last cans never took their place beside the small wooden box my father had carefully crafted to hold the last three seeds of each kind against any difficult Winter which might follow.

These three last cans we chose to give to others, less fortunate than we, along with some of the new corn. For they also lived within our House, within the larger House of our Great City.

"They need it more than we," he agreed, "for you see, they have no child within their small house with the wisdom to preserve this ocean Brother against a leaner Winter."

"Perhaps they also lack a father who explains such things," I suggested.

"Perhaps they do," he laughed. "And yet, perhaps one day all Earth's children will learn Third Winter wisdom . . and teach themselves how such things may be accomplished wherever they may be. Perhaps tuna fish needs to become one of our Sacred Sisters. Perhaps something quite else may be added. Even in the scarcest land, it seems to me, wisdom and love teach new possibilities . . love for each other . . love for the Earth.

"And perhaps one day we will all learn the value of sharing within the House . . and come to understand how Great that House may be."

I understood my father's words. For a Long House is built in such a manner that we need only add a little to its length in order to include new people.

"It was our thought .. that perhaps one day Earth's children would be wise enough to build so Great a House that its length would reach straight round this Earth and include us all as Brothers."

"As Sisters, too," I reminded.

And my Father smiled.

Many Circles,
Many Paths

Many Circles,
Many Paths

A Native American Learning Story

by Paula Underwood

It was dark in the clearing
    Only occasional fires
        lit the faces that surrounded them
    The night sky was overcast
        darkening even the stars

Many voices were heard here and there
    among the houses
Something
    was being discussed
        that no one at all
            found easily resolved

For a long time now
   Our strongest efforts
      had been of no benefit to our own People

We sought Deer
We gathered Corn
   as we knew how to do
Hung these useful gifts
   to the well-being of the People
      near the edge of our clearing . .

And suddenly
   a great noise and many running feet
      announced the arrival of a different People
         one living to the South
         one willing to take with shouts and threats
           what they were not willing
              to find for themselves

And Deer
Or Corn
   the gathered work of many People . .
      was gone in an instant
Carried South
   by an uncaring People

It had begun a different way

This Southern People
   arrived at the Circle of our Community
      and were welcomed as guests
What we had was shared

   It was our way

And yet this was not enough

   This People came . . . and came again
   So often guests
      that their labor for the common good
         was now invited

   This one and that from among our People
      would offer to show them
         our way with Deer and Corn

   "So that we may one day
      visit you with equal benefit"
         - - someone said

And yet
   None among them
      stepped forward to learn

Now
  There was at that time
    one among the People
      remarkable for his Patience

    No one but he
      was most easily learned from

And so it was
  We sent our children to him
      knowing that even the least willing among them . .
      would benefit from his attention

And so it was this one
  We asked now
      to help us with a different Learning . .

    How it was
      we might encourage this Visiting People
        to pay us fewer visits . .
      and to find their own well-being
        where they were

"It is like this"
  - - he answered us - -

"No one learns
   when they are not ready
I only wait for that time"

We saw how it was
   That both the patience for such waiting
      and the wisdom to recognize
         any sudden willingness to learn
            were equal in his nature
         both required for one
            who may be so easily learned from

And we honored him for this

And so it was
  That this Patient Watcher
    took on a special responsibility
      for the learning of this Southern People

  He travelled many days to the South
    so that he might learn
      the nature of their learning

Then at last
  He saw smoke rising from individual fires . .

  Moving slowly in that direction
    his path was suddenly barred
      by three from among that People
        carrying heavy spears

  He showed them his open hands
In neither one was any weapon

  And so it was
    That with great reluctance
      they finally let him pass

He made his careful way
  toward the rising evidence of fire ..
And found himself at last
  in the Circle of a different Community

One
  that showed by the manner of their sitting
    many divisions and few connections

A People
  whose distinctions divided them
    against each other - -
      setting this one against that

He saw in these sitting groups
  no pattern which wove them together
    connecting the differences
      into a general unity

      And he wondered much

He saw how it was
  that such a People would of their nature
  find new learning difficult

For surely
  New Learning . .
    shared by the Whole Community . .
      requires some continuing way of sharing

Here he saw none - -
  and wondered
    how his task of enabling their learning
      might yet be accomplished

For surely
  some agreement in general purpose
    was what our People sought

And surely
  that agreement
    however difficult to achieve
  was yet easier
    than many more years of disappearing Corn
    or than the strong work of defending it

And so it was
  That Patient Watcher
    began the slow work of threading connections
    between one People and another

As each Moon turned and left
   he moved from one Community to another
   watching - - as was his nature - -
   for the glimpses of light
      that precede a willingness to learn

And slowly
   this one and that from this new Community
   began to see some benefit in his purpose
   began to follow his path from time to time
   learning new ways of provision

For at last
  Some among them
    found some comfort in his presence
      some ease with his way of being

  They saw
    how it was
      that he brought with him what he needed to eat
        asking little at all of them

  They saw
    how his hands turned easily to their work
      never failing
        to render up what was asked of him

  They saw
    how he claimed nothing for himself
      but gave easily of all he had
        returning to his own Community
          for more, if necessary

  They saw
    how his Community had much
      as their Community had little

It was the wrong lesson

Now
  Patient Watcher
    kept a close eye and a gentle smile
      on all that transpired

He saw
  how this one and that
    was so comfortable in his presence
      that she felt no reason
        to change her manner
          when he arrived

It was his thought
  that it was time
    for the next learning

And so
  He took out the many seeds of Bean
    he had brought with him . .
  And began to find a place for each, here and there
    allowing them space to grow

  Neither did he place these seeds for Tomorrow
    in any regular field
  It was not his wish
    to seem to claim any space as his own

Rather
  he placed individual seeds here and there
    where they might flourish in isolation
      leaving the crop for Tomorrow

And some among the People
  asked his purpose . .
    which he explained
      as asking Earth to give us Beans Tomorrow

And among those who asked
  arose some understanding . .

So that
  This One or That
    began to watch in some patient way
      for green tendrils from a brown Earth

And the nature of this people
  Began to change

And yet
  Being who they were
    Tomorrow's bounty seemed a lack today . .

And
  although none dug up the earth-buried Beans . .
    some sought their source for today's plenty - -
    and returned with both Deer and Corn
      which none of them had first found . .
      and none of them had planted

Now
  Patient Watcher
    understood what this might mean

He understood
  his own People were streched beyond endurance . .
    providing nourishment
      not only for their own People
        but perhaps as much as half
          what was consumed
          by this Southern People as well

He saw
  it was time to return home

And
Surely as he thought it might be . .
even so
were his People discussing any plan at all
that might bring resolution

Some spoke for an agreement
whereby so much, but no more
might be given to this Southern People
for their comfort

But none could see
how such an agreement
might be achieved

Not even Patient Watcher

And
   Some spoke for a continuing defense
      of all we gathered
         from Earth's generosity . .

   But none could see
      how Deer and Berry might be gathered
         and also defended
   For it would require many of the People
      and constant vigilance
         to guard against such an aquisitive People

And all saw how this was so
   None were eager
      to undertake such night watches
         or such angry defense

   We saw how it would change the People
      and had no wish to see such changes

   And so
   Some spoke of a new learning
      for this Southern People

"Let us leave"
  - - someone suggested - -
    "A recently gathered Deer . .
      filled with some of the berries
        that cause great sickness

"Perhaps they will learn from this
  that our bounty may be unreliable

"Perhaps they will learn from this
  the wisdom of gathering their own Deer . . "

And he sat down
The consternation among the People was great - -
  this one and that spoke for a limiting sickness . .
    and none spoke against

Until at last
  Patient Watcher rose in his place . .
    and a willingness to listen to his words
      was followed by a great silence

127

"I have told you how it is"
  — he began —

"How these — our Southern Brothers —
  slowly begin to learn

"I have told you how it is
  That — over time — they will yet learn . .
    and come to gather even as we

"I see how it will be"
  — he went on —

"That they will then become our Brothers . .
  even as we understand them as Brothers now

"And yet I tell you
  This will not be soon"

  He stopped for a moment
    looking slowly around the Circle
      of his Community
  All eyes regarded him now
    even as all ears listened

"I see the impatience among you
I see many of your gatherings
  disappearing down a Southern Trail
Even that which goes with me
  in honor of some sought-for learning . .
    equally disappears down that same trail

"I see a willingness to share - -
  even to share our gathered Wisdom - -
    and I honor you for this

"Yet I see long days spent in too much effort
  long nights spent in sorrowing
    over that which is gone

"I see a People
  unwilling to spend that same effort on defense
  unwilling to become a People
    who has forgotten how to share

"And yet
  I also see a People
    unwilling to go hungry
      because others refuse to learn"

He paused again . .
  regarded the circle of questioning faces
    and sought some further understanding

"Our Brother
  has suggested the possibility
    of Deer which sickens

"I understand your impatience

"I understand this other People
  will take a long time to learn

"I understand your need
  to retain
    more of what you have gathered

"But I ask you to consider this . .

"If Deer is flavored with such berries . .
  where is the line
    between sickness and death?"

And
  Regarding the Circle of faces once more . .
    this Patient Watcher sat down

Now
  Discussion truly began

  For some from among the People
    still favored such a wounding Deer . .
  And others . . had no wish
    to become such a People

And so it was
  That impatience with slow learning
    caused so great a division
      among this united People
    that some of the Community moved North . .
      thinking to put too great a distance
        between them and the Southern People
          for any further insistence
            that we share what we had gathered

  But those of the Community who remained . .
    seeing that nothing at all
      prevented this Southern People
        from moving North as well . .
    decided to let Deer speak for them

They sent out scouts along the Southern trails
to bring warning . .
and gathered both Deer and Berries
against the possibility of such an arrival

And
When the scouts sent word
When Deer and Berries became one
When all was prepared in that way . .
the People began to leave their community . .
taking all but Deer with them

And
He who had patiently watched
all these preparations
stood again to speak

"You see how it is"
- - he said - -

"How I can neither leave this place
for a Northern Community . .
nor abandon it
to the hunger of this Southern People

"You see how it is"
  - - he went on - -

"How I have taken some responsibility
  for their learning . .
    and cannot now watch
      with any patience at all
        either their slow sickness
          or their sudden death

"You see how it is"
  - - he concluded - -

"How I will stay
  and will warn those who will listen
    that this is one Deer
      better left alone"

And so it was
   For no amount of encouragement
    from his People
       would dissuade him of his purpose
   He who valued Life and Learning
      above all else
         had no wish to end either for another People

And so - -
   Despite many warnings
      that this Southern People
         might be less patient with him
            than he with them . .
      he stayed
         even as the People left

      And waited patiently
       for the arrival
          of this Southern People

Now
This was the way of it . .

This Southern People arrived
hungry from their long walk
and from the little they found along the way

And they were greeted
by an abandoned Community . .
with one Deer laid out on the ground
and one man standing over him

Now
This man was one they recognized

Seen often among them and asking for little
they listened to him now - -
as he explained
the unity of Deer and Berries
saying this Deer had been left behind
as it was tainted - -
and would cause sickness . . or near death
for those who shared this apparent feast

And now
  the consternation
    of this Southern People began

For some said
  he meant to keep the Deer
    for himself
And others remembered
  his unending generosity

And some said
  he meant to protect Deer
    for his own People
And others remembered
  his invariable truthfulness

Until this community
  at last
    was divided
      even as ours had been

And
  Some cooked and ate this Deer

And others
  Sat with Patient Watcher
    in some wondering sorrow
      as the Deer
          quickly disappeared down as many throats
          as were willing to risk its nature

And
  Patient Watcher shared what little he had
    with those who sat with him . .

  And these were they
    who had begun to learn from him

So it was
  During this night —
    that the cries began

  Those who had quickly eaten . .
    as quickly died

  And those who had eaten little
    out of fear for what might be . .
      writhed now in anguish on the ground

  And those who saw possibility
    in the eyes of Patient Watcher
      these were they
        who cared for the sick and buried the dead

  For surely
    only those who had not eaten
      were well enough for this employ

And
   Patient Watcher wept . .

Wept at the impatience of his own People . .
   and at the unwillingness to learn
      of this Southern People also

"They have paid a great price
   for their foolishness"
      - - he pointed out - -

And
   all agreed it was so

My father's voice grew still, and my thoughts turned from one thing to another under his patient gaze.

"I can see how it is, my Father," I began at last "that we truly limit both ourselves and our understanding when we refuse to learn.

"I can see also how we limit our own learning when we refuse to listen to each voice.

"I can see how Patient Watcher waits for learning . . even as you wait for mine.

"And yet, you have not wept at my too-slow learning."

"It seems to me he weeps for something else," my father replied, "for his own foolishness and lack of understanding, for his inability to enable sufficient learning, for those who lay still against the Earth.

"Consider this also," he suggested. "What might have occurred had he given no warning?"

I saw before me the Circle of that community, none but one of the People any longer there.

I saw deer laid out upon Earth and sensed the presence of Berries. I saw a Southern People arrive in no small hunger . . and heard the words of Patient Watcher.

I saw some choose to build a fire and some choose to only watch - - I saw some eat with the relish of that hunger and some with hesitation.

I saw those who sat with Patient Watcher and saw how it was they did not eat at all. I saw . .

"They aren't eating," I explained as my startled eyes looked back at my father.

"And therefore . . ?" he asked in reply.

"And therefore there was more death than sickness! His warning *caused* the death of many! Had the sickening deer been equally eaten by all the Southern People - - perhaps none at all would have died.

"And Patient Watcher was wise enough to see this. This is why he wept! With his warning, he enabled great learning - - but the cost was great for those who refused to listen."

"Greatest of all in many ways for Patient Watcher," my father nodded. "For he truly understood the nature of his circumstance and the probable cost to those who would not learn.

"And from this he learned much"

Seeing my understanding eyes, my father's eyes turned slowly to the center of our own circle . .

And his voice began again . . .

Now
  This might be the end
    of one more Telling
     of Wisdom
        and Foolishness - -
       except that one more thing occurred

For
  Those who had begun
    to learn from
        Patient Watcher
     learned well that night . .
        and saw the value of their Learning

So
  When all was cleared away
    and those who had gone were gone
    and those who would stay were gathered . .

  This remnant of a Southern People
    called out to Patient Watcher . .
        and asked his attention

Now - -

They knelt before him . .
  And one who had been asked
    spoke for all

"We have watched you among us"
  - - she began - -

"We see how it is
    you are patient with our learning

 "We see how it is
    you share willingly
      anything you have gathered

 "We see how it is
    you trouble yourself about us
      again and again

"Yet we do not see why"

She paused . .
  and then went on

"We see now

"How you stayed to warn us
  of the nature of this Deer

  "Stayed with us
  even to help the sick and dying

"We see also
  that you ran great risk in this
    For no one assured your safety
      even as you sought to assure ours

"And yet
  We do not see why"

Again she paused . .
  and then continued

"So now we say this . .

    "You are our father

    "You are father to our learning

    "Even father to our life

    "For surely
        it would be gone
        but for you

"And
    We say this also . .

      "We are your children

      "From this day forward
        we will learn from none
        but you

      "Guide us
        our father"

And
　She settled herself on the Earth . .
　　become in her own right
　　　one more patient watcher

And
　He to Whom She Spoke
　　arose to give his answer . .

　"As you call me Father to your understanding
　　so do I call you Mother to mine . .
　　　For much has been learned here
　　　　and much will yet be learned

　"No one at all
　　is wise enough
　　　to lead another
　　　　without question

　"No one at all
　　is foolish enough
　　　to only follow

And so I say this . .

    "Let us make Community together
    "Let us learn from one another
    "Let us respect the differences we find
    "Let us learn to live together

    "For if I understood
      The nature of Brotherhood before
       I understand it better now . .

    "And see clearly each of you
      is Brother or Sister
      To my own being

    "Let us form together
      A new understanding
      of Community

    "Let us form together
      A new understanding
      of Patience. .
        one with the other

"Let those who will . .
   join us"

And it was so - -
   For when those
      who set Deer in such a visible place
         returned - -
   They found more
      than Patient Watcher
   And less
      than they had feared

And the many new furrows
   beyond the edge of the clearing
      spoke of what had happened

And . .
   By common agreement . .
      what had been two disparate Communities . .
         became three
            who understood the nature of cooperation
         three
            who learned from one another

For they understood
  how it was
    that each Community
      forms a circle

And how it was
  that these many circles on the Earth
    may learn from one another

They understood
  how it was
    that many paths
      may be traced on the Earth
        From one Community to the next . .

And some
  may be laid out by those
    who demand some benefit . .

And others
  by those
    who seek only to learn

And it seemed to them
they wanted . .
to be a Learning People

And
Patient Watcher
looked out from eyes
shaded by brows slowly turning white . .

and valued all learning . .
however slow, however fast

and learned himself . .
as is the way with such folk

During his Life
he was greatly honored
yet never would allow
the seating of one above another

151

And after his life
  had been fully spent in learning
    they remembered his Spirit
      and paid him great honor

In this manner
  they showed their respect
    for the nature of his being

And some say . .

  That
    when each of us
      shows a willingness
        to learn
          and
        to listen to our Brother

  We honor his Spirit still

Central Fire

For those who understand the meaning of Central Fire, there can be no explanation.

For those who not yet see the mounting flames calling the hunter from his forest, the farmer from her field, gathering the People to share their wisdom toward a shared decision . . . know that each Council Fire was lit as a beacon, forming the center toward which all faced. No one of the People was the Fire. Yet the Fire was their Center, their gathered energy mounting skyward, like their prayers, toward the Reality which lies beyond.

This shared focus was constructed by many hands, like the Long Houses in which they lived. To this beacon each one brought some wood, like food to the Central Feast. Out of unity, some greater purpose. What is impossible for one, many may yet accomplish.

Even in a summer's warmth, even in a small dwelling where any fire at all would have been intolerable, the Central Fire was still there . . . built by each hand, lit by the mind, by the heart, if not by any hand.

Like the Central Fire around which my Father and I always sat, fed by both hands, lit only by the heart, our Spirit dwelling, our round house, a white clapboard garage in a County that did not allow fire. Our expanding world a Circle of Two.

So did the Circle of the People face toward their Council Fire, lit whenever there was need, lit also at regular intervals to remind them of the continuing need for consensus, for unity of purpose. Individuality stood around the Council Circle, yet unity grew and changed in the Circle's Center, like the flames of the Council Fire.

"Let all leave behind their individual concerns, safe beyond the Circle. Let our thoughts draw toward our Center. Let us be warmed by our Common Purpose," some Elder would intone.

And so it was. I and you may differ, may fall to blows between us. Yet, if our thoughts turn toward the Center, I and you - - and as many others as there may be - - may yet build our Central Fire, create and sustain its energy, recognize our Common Purpose.

Let it be so.

On the Nature
of Learning Stories

You see how it is? How it is in the nature of many cultures to enable learning by telling stories?

In the Western world we remember Aesop's fables . . and their moral lessons. We remember folk tales . . and how they tell us to be honest, to be determined, to be generous. These tellings remind us of things we should remember . . things our culture, our society needs for general health.

Learning Stories are different.

Learning Stories are designed to engender questions, not to answer them — to raise issues, not to resolve them. They are an invitation to contemplation.

"Look how the world can be," they tell us. "Look what is here! If you were there then, instead of here now, what would your answer be?" they imply.

And so we feel ourselves oddly incomplete - - and yet complete.

Unanswered, yet filled with questions.

Such Tellings are not designed to teach a culture so much as they are designed to exercise the mind, the Spirit, the walk-around way each of us chooses.

Which path for you, my Brother, my Sister? Which path do you choose? I, who study with you, I choose this one! But which do you choose? And let us share our thoughts with one another as we each choose a path. Then we will both be wiser.

Such Tellings, such Learning Stories, enable us to learn from each other as much as we learn from the words, the images. They enable us to learn from our own wisdom, that which sometimes hides behind assumptions - - family assumptions, community assumptions. They liberate rather than define.

"Be . . all that you can be!" said a friend of mine who worked at the time for the Army.

Wonder . . about those possibilities.

This is the invitation that comes to each of us through any Learning Story. Explore, redefine, examine . . .

And if you lack Long Life Wisdom, you will therefore have New Eyes Wisdom, the gift of youth. Whatever your gift, apply it to the circumstance, this circumstance, every circumstance.

Let us learn together, my Brothers, my Sisters. Let us learn together, Grandfather, Grandmother, all Earth's children.

Let us learn together.

Weaving Wisdom From a Learning Story

When I first heard the Telling of *Wolf* from my Father, I was not yet three.

"What . . . may we learn from this?" he asked me.

In my best three-year-old parlance I answered, "Huh?"

"What do you think about when you hear this Story?"

"Ummm . . . Wuff!"

"Umm-hum . . . and what else?"

"Ummm . . . I dunno."

"Well," he replied with the beginnings of that infinite patience I came to value, "If you think of anything else . . . I'd like to hear about it."

So I thought about it. Wondered what learning was. Wondered what I might learn.

Finally, I decided I didn't really know the answer to either of these questions I asked myself. I decided I had to experience this Telling again - - or I would never learn these answers.

I went to my Father and began the first of my endless and repeated petitions. "Daddy . . . Wuff again?"

And he began the song.

Over the years, again and again I asked to hear one of the Tellings, so that I might learn. He shared them with me one more time . . . and then asked the ancient question.

When I learned the last lesson he was able to identify in *Wolf* I was 17 years old.

During these same years, he began to share with me the nature of symbolic learning, that which transcends the immediately logical. And at last I began to understand how much a true Learning Story might convey . . and in what manner.

So that you may witness on these pages some of the nature of my learning from my Father - - what he said, what I answered - - I have written down my memory of one of these exchanges . . . which took place *long* after the age of three.

"What may we learn from this?" my Father was asking, beginning the long dance between those who seek and those who beckon.

I looked up in surprise.

"This is a Learning Story?" I asked, startled, for where were the symbols of a broader reality?

"All Tellings may be learned from" he encouraged. "But surely for the People to have kept this one so long, it must contain some wisdom . . . . What do you see here?"

Searching the air for symbols finally I ventured, "Wolf, of course, and Fire . . . and Moon and Forest. Grandfather is witness to it all . . . and to the Boy's learning."

"Is Wolf not also witness?"

"Wolf is there to understand Fire . . . as Moon-Looking-Wolf seeks to understand Moon. Wolf-Looks-at-Fire does not seek to understand the People."

"Does not?" my Father asked.

But I understood his meaning. "He seeks to understand his relationship to Fire and the nature of Fire. Moon-Looking-Wolf seeks to understand the nature of Moon and many join her in her search, understanding thereby their relation to each other, understanding the People we call Wolf."

My father was pleased. His expression barely changed, but I felt his pleasure. His eyes turned to questions and I knew there was more to learn.

I thought of Moon and Wolf and Fire and saw at last the connection.

"Within the Circle of the People I see a form which has three sides. Wolf-Fire-Wolf," I described in the air, "Wolf-Fire-Boy. Each reaches out toward the other. Wolf and Boy seek understanding of Fire, are warmed by the nature of Fire. Each sees in the other's face a reflection of the nature of Fire and find between them a common curiosity.

"Other Wolf Persons explore the nature of Moon, see in her face a reflection of the reality that lies beyond." I paused and searched the images in my mind, each forming one point of the three-sided forms contained within the Circle of the People. I saw the fire in the reality which lies beyond. I saw Wolf . . and Wolf . . and Wolf regarding Moon. I saw Earth and Moon, both regarding that distant fire, both reflecting its warmth, and felt that same warmth on my face.

"We regard the Central Fire as our source of warmth, our common Center. Pulling us toward it, it encourages us toward each other."

"Is it any different for Wolf? That same Fire, that same reflection, arouses our desire to understand, to absorb within our being the reality of Fire, its nature, its flowing through Universe."

"No different," I said. "It is our nature to understand the Reality that lies beyond by watching its reflection in our Brother's face. And so, seeking understanding, Wolf and Boy are also brothers.

"Well, I will continue to consider the nature of Wolf and Boy and Fire. Of Grandfather and his quiet Joy in watching the reflection of understanding on the face of He of Eight Winters.

"I see that this is the foundation of the nature of the understanding of the People, a three-sided form within its circle, many three-sided forms, Person and Person, the Reality they regard, their relationship with each other."

I heard the Joy in my Father's voice.

"You understand the tap root of the meaning that our symbols touch, my Daughter. Do not let this understanding slip away!"

And so I sat for awhile, looking at Wolf and Moon, Boy and Grandfather, and always beyond some Central Fire.

Without moving, I danced circles around this Fire . . . and understood all three-sided forms, all Circles however large, however small, for such is the nature of understanding. Between fire spark and starshine a difference in size, no difference in nature.

I danced the patterns into my mind, remembering them as shapes against which to measure all future understanding. Turning and circling, treading now the arched path that contains the understanding, now the straight path of Perception, I danced to the beat of the Universe, danced to the tune of one Generation caring that the next may learn, danced to my Father's love flowing through me into the Future.

"Hey ya, Ya yo!" I intoned at last, in recognition of Spirit and of the Spirit Path.

"Hey ya, Ya yo, Hoy!" My Father replied, reinforcing with his heart my growing perception.

"We dance upon the Spirit path," he said, "understanding our own direction, understanding the spinning motion of all things, circles that are lines, lines that are circles."

We sang on and on until we were exhausted. Then sat, breathing slowly, until Spirit returned to sit within its Earth Center. And we looked . . . from one to the other, to the Central Fire we never lit, which was always there, and understood the nature of our mutual caring.

At last, I raised my head again and suggested, "There is more to be learned from this Telling, my Father. I see how the People gather around their Central Fire to reach mutual understanding. I see the relationship of different Peoples and the Earth they stand on, the limits and the largeness of Space, of Time . . ." I hesitated. My patterns in the air ceased their flow.

"I shall begin again," my Father offered . . . nothing but patience filled his voice.

He paused, drumming with his fingers on his knee, keeping the rhythm of the ancient chant.

"Almost at the edge of the Circle of light cast by Central Fire, Wolf was standing . . ."

162

164

THE AUTHOR — PAULA UNDERWOOD

Paula Underwood was author, speaker, trainer, and consultant in education, cross-cultural understanding and organizational methodologies. Paula's major written work came from the inherited responsibility for a consensual 10,000-year Oral History of her People handed down in her family through five generations. This record of a culture dedicated to learning was published in 1993 under the title: *The Walking People: A Native American Oral History.*

Paula authored The Three Learning Stories contained in this volume. The first of these, *Who Speaks for Wolf,* received the Thomas Jefferson Cup Award for quality writing for young people. It has been declared an Environmental Classic and called "The best book I know of on Systems Thinking". Most recently Paula published Vol. I of *The Great Hoop of Life: A Traditional Medicine Wheel for Enabling Learning and for Gathering Wisdom.* Her writings have been developed into an educational outreach program, The Past Is Prologue.

Throughout her life, Paula served her community. She grew up in Los Angeles; then spent 35 years in the Washington, D.C. area where she earned an M.S. in International Relations, worked on Capitol Hill and as an active volunteer with The League of Women Voters. She has served on boards of organizations oriented toward learning and the environment. In 1989 she moved to Marin County, CA, to devote over a decade to her writing and to devise ways to share her unique heritage with "those who would listen." During this period she founded and directed a non-profit organization, The LearningWay Center which continues to support Paula's work. Since her death in 2000, Paula's two children, Randy Spencer and Laurie Spencer Roberts, are continuing The Tribe of Two Press.

Paula cited her Ancestors as believing: ". . . learning is so valuable . . that it is therefore sacred." Her writings serve to honor the beauty of such a Life.

THE ARTIST — FRANK HOWELL

Frank Howell is best known for his intricately detailed renderings of American Indians. He viewed these works as universal symbols — as a kind of visual mythology. A mid-westerner by birth, he spent many years in the Santa Fe and Denver areas where he became nationally known not only for his acrylics and oils but also for his lithographs, monotypes, watercolors, drawings and sculpture. He taught on both high school and college levels. Before his death he wrote several books and illustrated many others.

Books by Paula Underwood
Available from A Tribe of Two Press

Three Strands in the Braid: A Guide for Enablers of Learning
Designed to be used with The Three Learning Stories: *Who Speaks for Wolf, Winter White and Summer Gold,* and *Many Circles, Many Paths,* now published in one volume as *Three Native American Learning Stories.* There is also available an audio cassette with Paula Underwood reading *The Three Learning Stories.*

The Walking People: A Native American Oral History
(Published in collaboration with the Institute for Noetic Sciences)
The saga of Paula Underwood's People and the Learnings and Wisdom they gathered as they walked from their Edge of Ocean home in Asia across the Bering Strait, across the continent of what they called Turtle Island, at last finding a home for the Children's, Children's, Children in the woodlands of Northeast America.

The Great Hoop of Life, Volume I: A Traditional Medicine Wheel for Enabling Learning and for Gathering Wisdom
A Learning Tool designed to help with the tasks of conceptualization, organization of new information. and sustainable decision making.

Franklin Listens When I Speak: Tellings of the Friendship between Benjamin Franklin and Skenandoah, an Oneida Chief
Paula Underwood's ancestry includes stories handed down from her Oneida spiritual grandmother, Tsilikoma, but also from her blood grandmother from the Folger line on her paternal grandmother's side, giving her an unusual perspective on American history.

My Father and the Lima Beans
A small pamphlet with one of the many stories Paula's father told her to point out the value of community building. Paula frequently used this story as an effective tool for the corporate workshops she initiated.

Books may be ordered directly from
A Tribe of Two Press
P.O. Box 133, Bayfield, CO 81122
Phone: 1-800-995-3320
Website: www.tribeoftwopress.com